MULTIPOINT FEEDBACK

A 360° Catalyst for Change

Deborah Jude-York, Ph.D.
Susan L. Wise, M.A.

A FIFTY-MINUTE™ SERIES BOOK

CRISP PUBLICATIONS, INC.
Menlo Park, California

MULTIPOINT FEEDBACK
A 360° Catalyst for Change

Deborah Jude-York, Ph.D.
Susan L. Wise, M.A.

CREDITS
Managing Editor: **Kathleen Barcos**
Editor: **Andrea Reider**
Production: **Leslie Power**
Typesetting: **ExecuStaff**
Cover Design: **Carol Harris**

All rights reserved. No part of this book may be reproduced or transmitted in any form or by any means now known or to be invented, electronic or mechanical, including photocopying, recording, or by any information storage or retrieval system without written permission from the author or publisher, except for the brief inclusion of quotations in a review.

Copyright © 1997 by Crisp Publications, Inc.

Printed in the United States of America by Bawden Printing Company.

Distribution to the U.S. Trade:

National Book Network, Inc.
4720 Boston Way
Lanham, MD 20706
1-800-462-6420

Library of Congress Catalog Card Number 96-72562
Jude-York, Deborah and Susan L. Wise
Multipoint Feedback
ISBN 1-56052-427-8

This book is printed on recyclable paper with soy ink.

LEARNING OBJECTIVES FOR:

MULTIPOINT FEEDBACK

The objectives for *Multipoint Feeback* are listed below. They have been developed to guide you, the reader, to the core issues covered in this book.

Objectives

☐ **1)** To explain multipoint feedback and its usefulness.

☐ **2)** To show how to administer multi-point feedback.

☐ **3)** To explain the mechanics of a multipoint feedback survey.

☐ **4)** To discuss evaluation and implementation of a multipoint feedback survey.

Assessing Your Progress

In addition to the Learning Objectives, *Multipoint Feedback* includes a unique new **assessment tool*** which can be found at the back of this book. A twenty-five item, multiple choice/true-false questionnaire allows the reader to evaluate his or her comprehension of the subject matter covered. An answer sheet, with a chart matching the questions to the listed objectives, is also provided.

* Assessments should not be used in any selection process.

ABOUT THE SERIES

With over 200 titles in print, the acclaimed Crisp 50-Minute™ series presents self-paced learning at its easiest and best. These comprehensive self-study books for business or personal use are filled with exercises, activities, assessments, and case studies that capture your interest and increase your understanding.

Other Crisp products, based on the 50-Minute books, are available in a variety of learning style formats for both individual and group study, including audio, video, CD-ROM, and computer-based training.

ABOUT THE AUTHORS

Deborah Jude-York, Ph.D.—Deborah has over 20 years experience in Human and Organizational Development in health care, manufacturing, high tech, and telecommunications. She is the Managing Partner of The York Consulting Team, a company specializing in designing large-system culture change interventions, working with organizational leaders and managers to custom-design Multipoint Feedback interventions, including survey design, report preparation, meeting facilitation, and follow-up coaching. Their clients include IBM, Pacific Bell, Pacific Telesis, The Clorox Company, Kaiser Permanente, and PG&E.

Susan L. Wise, M.A.—Susan is an Organization Development consultant currently with Pacific Bell, specializing in the area of Multipoint Feedback, teambuilding, workforce planning, and employee satisfaction initiatives. She holds her master's degree in Organizational Psychology from Saint Mary's College of California.

CONTENTS

INTRODUCTION vii

PART I   UNDERSTANDING MULTIPOINT FEEDBACK 1
         Defining Multipoint Feedback 3
         Why Organizations Use Multipoint Feedback 5
         A Catalyst for Change 8
         Catalytic Change 10

PART II   EVERYONE BENEFITS 13
          Preparation 15
          Setting Your Own Objectives 16
          Assessing Readiness 17
          Critical Success Factors 18
          Red Flags 19

PART III   PROCESS OVERVIEW 21
           Roles and Responsibilities 23
           Key Decision Points 25
           Introduction to Case Study 29
           Timeline Planning Chart 30

PART IV   MULTIPOINT FEEDBACK: A TEN-STEP JOURNEY 31
          #1: Determining Your Picture of Successful
              Leadership and Teamwork 33
          #2: Developing Your Multipoint Feedback Survey 36
          #3: Choosing Your Feedback Team 44
          #4: Holding a Kick-Off Meeting 46

PART V   THE FEEDBACK LOOP 49
         #5: Survey Distribution 51
         #6: Report Preparation 53
         #7: Interpreting Your Multipoint Feedback Report 59
         #8: Holding Team Feedback Meetings With Your
             Direct Reports 70

CONTENTS (continued)

PART VI   **COMPLETING THE PROCESS** 77

                  #9: Developing Your Action Plan 79

                  #10: Commitment to Next Steps and Follow-Up 81

PART VII   **TEST YOUR LEARNING** 85

                  Multipoint Feedback Crossword Puzzle 87

ASSESSMENT

INTRODUCTION

The concept of Multipoint Feedback is stimulating a lot of interest and attention in business today. There is a good reason for this! As individuals and organizations continually change and grow, information becomes the most powerful resource a person can have. Multipoint Feedback is an information-rich tool that solicits direct and specific data from key individuals, with the potential to produce a high degree of individual and organizational change. In essence, Multipoint Feedback is to individual and organizational change what the Internet is to the information superhighway. As a tool, Multipoint Feedback is information. As a process, Multipoint Feedback is a catalyst for change.

Because an organization is defined by the individuals who make it up, this book will focus on the what, why, and how of Multipoint Feedback. For the individual employee, this book will enable you to get valuable feedback from those with whom you work: your manager, peers, customers, and direct reports who will see you and your performance from their unique perspectives. Multipoint Feedback will prepare you to lead your team through a sea of change—knowing everyone has a life jacket!

The objective of a Multipoint Feedback process is to improve the competencies, skills, and behaviors of a single person or a collection of individuals. A standard set of competencies are developed and individuals are assessed and given feedback against the common set. Peers, customers, direct reports, and a person's manager all give feedback to an individual using the same set of questions. Occasionally, there may be a few extra questions added specifically for one group or another. Many people add about ten questions of their own, geared towards their direct reports which usually address specific coaching, managing, or team-building behaviors.

Place a check (✔) next to the items that stimulate your interest in Multipoint Feedback:

❏ I am interested in improving my leadership skills.

❏ I don't currently supervise a team of employees but I would like to receive feedback from others, such as my peers, my customers, and my manager.

❏ My boss suggested that I improve how I manage people.

INTRODUCTION (continued)

❑ I am being considered for a promotion and would like to (or am being requested to) receive feedback from others to confirm my readiness.

❑ I have heard a lot of people talking about Multipoint Feedback and would like to learn more about it.

❑ I work in a company where others are participating in Multipoint Feedback and I am interested in learning more about it before I am required to participate.

❑ I have been asked to set up a Multipoint Feedback program as part of my job.

❑ I am a student and want to learn more about Multipoint Feedback.

❑ I participated in Multipoint Feedback in the past and would like to understand other options and success factors.

Amongst the greatest challenges facing business leaders today is creating an environment that allows change management to occur and become an ongoing process to improve business performance. It is particularly complex because the change needs to start with the leader!

The techniques and tools covered in this book have proven to be very effective in helping me and my leadership team become more contemporary leaders. Properly applied and periodically reinforced, these tools can help organizations perform substantially better in a sustainable manner.

I am a strong believer in using 360° feedback as a catalyst for change.

—Thomas G. Cross
  Vice President Organizational Development
  Pacific Bell

PART

I

Understanding Multipoint Feedback

DEFINING MULTIPOINT FEEDBACK

Feedback is:

the process of communicating to another individual how you perceive (feel, believe, think) they perform their job and/or how effective they are in working with you in your job.

Multipoint Feedback is:

the process of obtaining feedback from multiple individuals, a 360° view from those who are directly affected by the way you perform your job, people who work with you or for you, and the people you work for, either your manager or your customers.

Full Circle Feedback

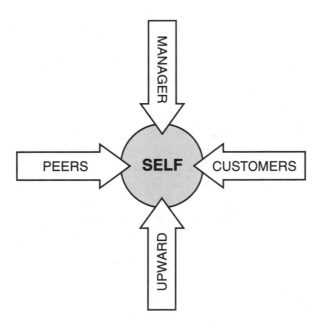

DEFINING MULTIPOINT FEEDBACK
(continued)

Multipoint Feedback comes from:

► **Your Manager**   Providing feedback on how your performance meets his/her expectations and the requirements of your job.

► **Your Peers**   Giving you professional or technical insight about your performance and ability to influence overall business objectives, and how working with you enhances or detracts from their ability to be effective in their role.

► **Your Customers**   Providing feedback on how well your performance meets their expectations and enables them to serve their own customers effectively. Internal customers are others who work inside your company. They receive the products, data, and information that you produce at work. In this book, we will refer to internal customers as your *customers.* In other cases, some people may choose to solicit feedback from *external* customers, the people outside your organization to whom you sell products and services.

► **Your Direct Reports**   Providing suggestions for how you could be more effective in leading, coaching, and supporting their work, and validating the things you currently do well. Direct reports will provide Upward Feedback for you.

► **Your Self**   Examining your perceptions of your own strengths and opportunity areas.

WHY ORGANIZATIONS USE MULTIPOINT FEEDBACK

TEAM BUILDING

Getting people to work effectively with each other is always an ongoing management challenge. A Multipoint Feedback process helps to identify commonly agreed-upon leadership behaviors that, when done well by each member, results in successful team performance. It provides each team member with the opportunity to give feedback to their peers within a safe and comfortable process. Although we would like to believe that we are open to providing and receiving feedback from one another as a matter of daily practice, this is rarely the case. Under the umbrella of a Multipoint Feedback process, telling others how their behaviors and actions affect us becomes a legitimate and expected behavior.

TRAINING NEEDS ASSESSMENT

Training employees is one of the most important and expensive human resource interventions an organization provides. Adults learn most effectively when the subject to be studied is critical and relevant to their current performance challenges. Trainers want to target their teaching efforts where they can be most effective in closing knowledge and skill gaps in the areas where employees may be performing below optimal levels. Multipoint Feedback summary results can help to identify critical performance gaps and suggest opportunities where training could significantly improve business results.

PERFORMANCE FEEDBACK

Many leaders struggle when they spend a large amount of time working with low-performing or problem employees. A great deal of time can be wasted in work teams when the focus on work gets distorted by non-productive and disruptive teammates. Hallway conversations consumed with negative discussions also result in a significant energy drain. Multipoint Feedback helps point out troublesome issues, and enables a manager to coach and redirect problem performers. Team members and customers have a recognized opportunity to give critical feedback to help their peers become more positive contributors.

WHY ORGANIZATIONS USE MULTIPOINT FEEDBACK (continued)

PROMOTION AND SUCCESSION PLANNING

Organizational leaders play a crucial role in guiding the work efforts of many people. Individuals who are placed in supervisory roles communicate behaviors and actions which are valued by top leadership. In other words, who gets hired sends a strong message to the employees about what is valued in a leader. In fact, it is the single strongest signal that can be sent and, therefore, warrants a carefully thought-out decision. In succession planning, early rounds of Multipoint Feedback can help candidates develop their weaker areas into strengths. Multipoint Feedback obtained for potential candidates who are aspiring for leadership positions can provide the business with additional insight on who might be the best candidate for the job.

MANAGEMENT DEVELOPMENT

As a management development tool, Multipoint Feedback provides individuals with insights that help increase their self-awareness and motivation for learning and developing in new ways. Many successful management training programs begin with a Multipoint Feedback process to help participants target their learning objectives in critical areas. Often Multipoint Feedback at the start helps participants to become more open and focused in their learning efforts. We often assume that attending a credible management training seminar will automatically result in each individual learning exactly the new skills, behaviors, and competencies that their peers, manager, and customers would want them to learn. Unfortunately, this rarely occurs, and attending management training often does not result in visible behavioral changes. Multipoint Feedback helps to connect customer requirements with management training and performance improvement expectations. Even more improvements occur when a second round of Multipoint Feedback is done several months after the training occurs to assess and affirm progress.

ORGANIZATIONAL CULTURE CHANGE

What is valued and important inside an organization is communicated informally by the organization's *culture*. Culture is represented by a set of values, beliefs, and behaviors that are acknowledged as positive by organizational leadership, creating the kind of work environment needed to position the company for future success. Changing the culture of an organization requires a clear picture of what the future company needs to look like. This is conveyed by the questions asked on the Multipoint Feedback survey. Motivation to change individual behaviors and actions (highlighted by the gap between ideal and actual scores), and a clear set of concrete do-able next steps is obtained during the team feedback meetings and action-planning process.

LEADERSHIP ALIGNMENT

When an organization wants to ensure that all of its employees and work efforts are pulling in the same direction, a Multipoint Feedback process establishes a common list of desired behaviors and actions against which individual performance is assessed. Each time an individual receives feedback through this model they become more aware of how closely their actions align with the expectations of others. Most people are motivated to learn and act, and to ensure they are being seen at the same level of performance, if not higher, than their peers.

A CATALYST FOR CHANGE

We believe that the majority of people approach their work wanting to do a good job and wanting others to feel good about working with them. Most of us have no idea how our behavior is seen or experienced by others. We generally do not go around giving each other unsolicited feedback on how well we see them do their jobs, or on how effective they are in working with us. While we may be consciously aware of many of our actions, such as assuming a leadership role when no one seems able to move, there are just as many things that we do out of habit and unconscious action. These represent our blind spots, areas of our private self which cause us to act without thinking. Although they are not a part of our conscious thinking and planning, these behaviors can be quite visible and impactful on others. The following Expanding Interpersonal Awareness model helps to show how the Multipoint Feedback process can increase self awareness and understanding of how we interact with others.

Expanding Interpersonal Awareness with Full Circle Feedback

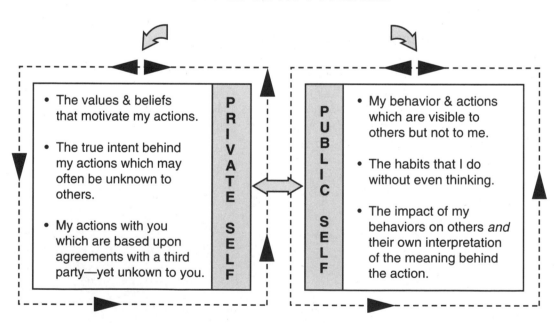

PRIVATE SELF

- The values & beliefs that motivate my actions.

- The true intent behind my actions which may often be unknown to others.

- My actions with you which are based upon agreements with a third party—yet unkown to you.

PUBLIC SELF

- My behavior & actions which are visible to others but not to me.

- The habits that I do without even thinking.

- The impact of my behaviors on others *and* their own interpretation of the meaning behind the action.

A simple formula for change demonstrates how and why Multipoint Feedback is an extremely effective tool in motivating action and personal change.

Expanding Interpersonal Awareness Model

$$(P + F + N) > I = C$$

P = Significant pain or displeasure with the current situation. Others are not happy with me and there is some degree of pressure on me to improve this.

F = A clear picture of how things could or should look in the future. The feedback survey describes specific behaviors and action. A really high set of scores would describe the ideal picture.

N = Clear, concrete next steps, or first steps, that will help you move from where you are today toward your ideal picture.

I = Inertia or lack of energy. We are all the most comfortable staying the way we are unless there is a strong enough push to cause us to move.

C = Change. Actually changing our behaviors or actions.

A combination of pain or discomfort, along with a clear picture of how it would look if things were different, plus some specific next steps, frequently enables us to overcome our natural tendency to remain as we are without changing.

CATALYTIC CHANGE

When we receive feedback from others we have a choice about whether to pay attention to or to discard it. We are more likely to acknowledge the feedback if we value the opinions of the people who are giving it to us, and if we believe that the questions are important. Most of the time we are not even aware that some of the things we do have an adverse affect on others at work.

Simply calling attention to the consequences of our actions can often be enough to motivate us to change. However, if the behaviors have become long-term habits, we will have to increase our self-awareness, in order to notice when we are engaging in the action under question. Most likely, we will catch ourselves after we have done it once again. Don't be surprised if you find yourself doing this over and over again. It takes time and energy to change behaviors and habits.

Once we are able to do things differently, there is often a lag time before others begin to notice. If after some time we do not receive positive reinforcement for our changes, it is easy to revert back to our old ways. Sometimes people are so used to how we used to act that they have a hard time noticing that we are no longer acting that way.

Positive reinforcement from others helps new behaviors stick and become a part of who we are and how we work. Change of this sort does not come easily. Open discussions can do a lot to clarify the intent behind our actions, and the *impact* of our behaviors on others. The Catalytic Change model on the next page helps to clarify this process of feedback and behavior change.

Catalytic Change Model

Decision not to change

- Contract to not act on feedback
- Re-negotiate expectations
- Explore Alternatives
- Do nothing and hope the need goes away

Feedback from Others

Awareness
- Personal acknowledgement that others would like me to change

Understanding
- Develop a clear picture of what desired behavior looks like and what undesirable behavior has looked like
- Understanding the consequences of my previous behavior on others
- Self-reflection: Exploring what has been driving my behavior in the past

Commitment
- Contract with others to change my behavior
- Ask for ongoing feedback and support

Experimentation
- Testing out new behaviors

Negative consequences or lack of notice → Revert to previous behavior

Validation

Assimilation
- Permanent adoption of the new behaviors
- Acknowledgement from others that my new behavior is noticed and appriciated

Continual Personal Growth

© 1995 Deborah Jude-York

Feedback from others can help to change our behaviors when we decide to do so, and in return we receive reinforcement for our efforts.

P A R T

II

Everyone Benefits

PREPARATION

When embarking on a Multipoint Feedback process it is important to think about your objectives in participating. Below are some objectives to consider:

For the Supervising Manager

► To identify specific leadership and team-building behaviors that can positively impact your team's performance or reverse negative trends.

► To develop specific action plans for improving leadership and individual behaviors that can improve team performance.

For the Team

► To increase openness and communication among team members.

► To increase accountability of team members in sharing responsibility for improvement with their manager.

► To realign team focus around critical goals and objectives. Stay away from "blaming the boss" discussions.

For the Organization

► An opportunity to align leadership and team behaviors for optimum performance.

► A catalyst to move toward an organizational culture that values open communication, team collaboration, and commitment to organizational goals.

For the Customer

► A chance to reinforce what is already valued, by providing reinforcing feedback.

► An opportunity to state requests for alterations and improvements.

SETTING YOUR OWN OBJECTIVES

EXERCISE: List the objectives or results you would like to gain from your own Multipoint Feedback process.

1. _____

_____

2. _____

_____

3. _____

_____

4. _____

_____

ASSESSING READINESS

An important step in beginning a Multipoint Feedback process is to honestly assess from what point you are starting so you can better determine the direction you are headed. Please place a check (✔) in the Low, Medium, or High box to indicate you current interests, feelings, and needs.

	LOW	MEDIUM	HIGH
1. I am open to hearing how my actions affect others.	❏	❏	❏
2. I value input from those who work with me.	❏	❏	❏
3. I can listen to feedback from others without getting defensive.	❏	❏	❏
4. I believe I could be a more effective manager.	❏	❏	❏
5. I can agree not to retaliate for people telling me the truth as they see it.	❏	❏	❏
6. I am willing to accept the perceptions others have of my performance, even if I do not agree with them.	❏	❏	❏
7. I welcome honest and direct feedback.	❏	❏	❏
8. I understand that the intent behind my behavior may not be what others actually experience.	❏	❏	❏
9. If I think the survey is asking the right questions, I will value the feedback.	❏	❏	❏
10. I recognize that in order to improve my leadership, I must be willing to take action on the feedback.	❏	❏	❏

If you scored yourself Low in three or more boxes, take the quiz again after you have finished reading this book. If your scores are still low, you may not be ready to proceed with Multipoint Feedback at this time. This process does require that you have some motivation to change and grow, as well as the willingness to receive feedback from others and be self-directed with your own development.

CRITICAL SUCCESS FACTORS

The *Multipoint Feedback Process* Must:

► Clarify issues about how the final feedback report will be used, such as developmental or evaluative, confidential or shared, anonymous, or names on surveys (See Part III for a discussion on the pro's and con's of each of these choices).

► Solicit feedback from individuals who have worked with you for at least four to six months.

► Be sure the people you ask to provide feedback are capable of answering the survey questions. They should have knowledge of your behaviors and actions in the situations addressed by your questions.

► Ensure that all participants who will be asked to give feedback know what to expect, and what will happen with their feedback.

► Include a combination of numerical and written summarized feedback in the Multipoint Feedback report.

► Include a way to follow-up with those who provide feedback.

► Include an action-planning step with identified areas to improve.

► Include a step for repeating the feedback in nine to twelve months.

The *Multipoint Feedback Survey* Must:

► Include questions that match your organization's vision, values, and goals.

► Include questions that measure appropriate competencies, behaviors, or skills.

► Ensure that the questions being asked are important, understandable, and meaningful to those being assessed.

► Ensure that those asked to provide feedback are capable of answering the survey questions; that they have had the opportunity to observe you in various leadership situations.

► Include questions that address a single behavior, so that others are not confused by multiple possibilities in how they interpret the questions.

RED FLAGS

The following situations are likely to result in trouble. Check (✔) any that apply to you, and either resolve them or **proceed with extreme caution.**

❏ I really do not want to participate in Multipoint Feedback; my boss is making me do it.

❏ I have a lot of people angry at me at the present time and I feel that they are likely to take it out on me with Multipoint Feedback.

❏ I work with a group of people that I really do not respect nor do I believe they are qualified to give me feedback.

❏ I already know what people think of me and I honestly do not intend to change.

❏ My organization is about to go through a big change (such as a merger or downsizing) and the new leadership will probably value a different set of leadership traits.

❏ I have been accused of discrimination, sexual harassment, or other misconduct that is likely to show up on my Multipoint Feedback.

❏ My boss would like to fire me and wants me to receive Multipoint Feedback to gather a case against me.

❏ Multipoint Feedback has been attempted before in my team and was misused.

If you made it through these, continue on to find out more about Multipoint Feedback.

III

Process Overview

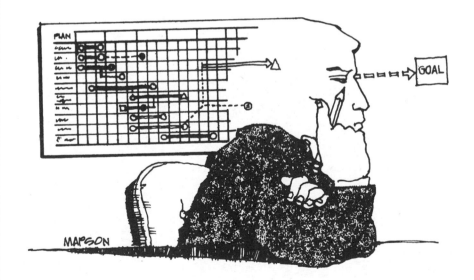

ROLES AND RESPONSIBILITIES

Your Role

As the manager who is requesting Multipoint Feedback, your role is to:

- Spend some time in the beginning planning out the process steps and making choices about your survey, such as who to request feedback from, and what you intend to do with the results when you get them back.

- Develop a timeline and inform all of those who will be participating when they can expect to receive the survey, when it needs to be returned, and what you hope to do with the results.

- Remain open to the inputs, views, and suggestions that others are willing to share with you. Ask questions, listen, and try to understand what it looks like from their points of view. Avoid being defensive and punishing others for being honest with you.

- Complete a self assessment.

- Develop an action plan and stick to your commitments.

- Seek additional feedback whenever you would like more specific information from others and follow up with another round of about Multipoint Feedback within nine to twelve months.

Feedback Providers' Roles

As a manager requesting Multipoint Feedback you should share or discuss this with those you will be soliciting feedback from.

As a feedback provider in a Multipoint Feedback, your role is to:

- Complete the survey as honestly and completely as you can.

- Fill in the examples or comments sections, (you may increase their understanding by providing specific examples or suggestions).

- Turn in the survey on time.

- Participate in feedback discussions sharing specific suggestions for what success would look like to you.

- Avoid hallway talk with others outside your group. This will protect the confidentiality of your feedback meeting.

- Give your manager positive reinforcement for all behavior change and alert your manager quickly when s/he falls off-the-track with your agreements.

ROLES AND RESPONSIBILITIES (continued)

Neutral Third Party Coach

Optional, but recommended.

Facilitating a Multipoint Feedback process is often more successful with the assistance of an experienced, neutral, and confidential coach. The coach plays an important role in helping a manager understand data and in helping the participating employees feel safe during the team feedback session.

Coaches often:

- Ask clarifying questions to stimulate a manager's understanding of the results.

- Share models to help the manager understand patterns and themes in the data.

- Observe and reflect behaviors that might be represented in the data.

- Provide support and encouragement for all participants.

- Help a manager to see how his/her strengths can be leveraged to develop his/her opportunity areas.

- Offer options for improvement and development.

- Assist the manager in accepting accountability for his/her results.

- Assist the manager in planning and designing an effective kickoff and team feedback meeting.

- Facilitate the manager's team feedback meeting, soliciting information on specific behaviors that led to strengths and behaviors which would lead to specific opportunities becoming future strengths.

The table on the followng pages details key decision points, your options, and considerations for implementing a Multipoint Feedback process.

KEY DECISION POINTS

DECISION POINTS	OPTIONS	CONSIDERATIONS
Survey	• Standard • Custom	Standardized surveys can be purchased from a variety of vendors and will require very little preparation time. They often come with access to large pools of scores which enable you to see how others have been scored on the same questions. Customized instruments measure exactly the attributes you want to develop in your organization. You can compare scores with organizational norms or with others who are participating in the Multipoint Feedback process.
Frequency	• Once per year • Twice per year • Every eighteen months	It is important to think about Multipoint Feedback as an ongoing process rather than a single event. Having subsequent rounds of feedback will validate changes made and encourage continuous improvement. Repeating the process in less than six months usually does not give you enough time to successfully and visibly change your behavior. Eighteen months, however, is often too long of a window to motivate action.
Confidentiality	• Participating manager • Participating manager and his/her boss • Shared with everyone who contributes	It is important to give some thought to how and who will see your feedback report before starting. While we like to encourage open sharing, there are some risks to consider. People who are asked to give feedback are more likely to be honest and open if they believe there will not be

KEY DECISION POINTS (continued)

DECISION POINTS	OPTIONS	CONSIDERATIONS
		harsh consequences for their boss or colleague. If the report will be shared with anyone other than the Multipoint Feedback candidate this should be made clear at the start. While it is not necessary to share the actual report with those who have given input, we encourage open discussion regarding the results and the path forward.
Accountability	• Developmental • Evaluative	The intent of the Multipoint Feedback should be made clear at the start. Will the results be used for personal and professional development only, or will there be consequences on a performance appraisal? We suggest that the first several rounds be developmental only and that eventually Multipoint Feedback becomes a voice on the performance appraisal. If Multipoint Feedback remains inconsequential over time, it becomes hard to take it seriously, especially among other pressing priorities.
Participation	Voluntary, or Mandatory	Generally most people get more out of Multipoint Feedback when they opt to participate on their own. We suggest that managers set an expectation that all will participate, allowing for some to start quickly and others to participate as they are ready. Fear and resistance may inhibit some from engaging, and they tend to get more comfortable watching others go first.

DECISION POINTS	OPTIONS	CONSIDERATIONS
Facilitation	Self-facilitation, or Facilitator from within the team or Outside facilitation	Even the most skilled managers who frequently facilitate meetings for others may find it challenging to preside over their own Multi point Team Feedback Meetings. It is not a question of skill but rather *role* and acceptance by others for positioning the discussion and responding to the feedback. A skilled, neutral facilitator can help both the manager and his/ her team hear one another. They also provide a safety net to ensure that the discussion does not get out of control and cause someone damage. Outside facilitators are more removed, neutral, and objective. They are not likely to be asked to share confidential information, or to show up in another working relationship down the road.
Reports	Process them yourself, or Ask or hire someone else	Processing the feedback instruments into a collated report is best done by someone other than the person requesting the feedback. This will allow the individual employees who gave feedback to remain anonymous. In general, people are more willing to be honest (although they may not like to admit this) when their anonymity is assured. The data can then be represented as average scores or ranges with synthesized or verbatim comments.

You will see references to a case study describing a regional sales account manager, Pauline Niner, in the following sections.

INTRODUCTION TO CASE STUDY

Pauline Niner

Pauline is a manager in a large organization where there has been a lot of talk about the Multipoint Feedback process. She is beginning her eighth year with the company and was recently promoted because of her consistent and outstanding sales results.

Pauline would like to jumpstart her own feedback process since her part of the organization is not scheduled for another five months. While Pauline believes that her own abilities to produce results are quite satisfactory, she has concerns about the productivity levels of several members of her direct report team. She would like to learn how to be more effective in motivating others and in building a strong team of sales account managers.

People who work with Pauline admire her success. They also have concerns about her effectiveness as a leader. Some people have overheard conversations where Pauline's direct reports speak critically of some of her behaviors. Pauline often seems rushed, and highly focused on attaining results. She rarely eats in the cafeteria and stays in her office most of the time. Pauline's customers love her, which is evidenced by her high achievements in exceeding sales challenges.

As you read on, you can follow Pauline and learn how she uses the Multipoint Feedback process to build her team and improve her leadership.

TIMELINE PLANNING CHART

As you continue through the remainder of this book, it will be helpful to consider the amount of time it might take to implement a Multipoint Feedback process. Below you will find a timeline to follow or modify depending on your needs. Advance planning will allow you to schedule your kick-off meeting and team-feedback meeting in advance to ensure the availability of your feedback team. Your timeline will vary based upon:

- Previous experience with and/or learning about Multipoint Feedback.

- The readiness of your feedback team for Multipoint Feedback.

- The work you may have already completed concerning the initial process steps.

- Your own sense of urgency and the ability of others to match.

PROCESS STEPS	TENTATIVE TIMELINE (WEEKS)	YOUR OWN TIMELINE
#1 Creating a picture of Successful Leadership	1–2	
#2 Developing Your Own Survey	3–4	
#3 Choosing Your Feedback Team	4	
#4 Holding a Kick-Off Meeting	5–6	
#5 Survey Distribution	5–6	
#6 Survey Return and Report Preparation	6–8	
#7 Reviewing your Feedback	9	
#8 Holding your Team Feedback Meeting	10	
#9 Developing an Action Plan	10–11	
#10 Next Steps and Follow-Up	10–11	
Total time to complete process	$2\,^1/_2$ mos.	

IV

Multipoint Feedback: A Ten-Step Journey

#1: CREATING A PICTURE OF SUCCESSFUL LEADERSHIP

If you are an individual manager or small team wanting to participate in a Multipoint Feedback process, it is important to consider and discuss the leadership model you believe is needed to be successful in the coming years. Be sure to look forward here—most likely some characteristics that were valued in the past will be changing in response to new developments in the marketplace. This leadership model is the foundation for building or choosing the Multipoint Feedback Survey which will best meet your needs.

Key Questions

What are the critical leadership behaviors that are needed for your business to be competitive today and during the coming years? Try to think about this from the following four viewpoints: your business, your customers, your employees, and what you read about changes in the marketplace.

If you are having trouble thinking about the various behaviors needed to be successful in your job and/or organization, the following exercise may be helpful to you.

#1: CREATING A PICTURE OF SUCCESSFUL LEADERSHIP (continued)

EXERCISE: Pick and choose from the following list of leadership characteristics needed to help your organization be successful today and in the future. Add more of your own thoughts if you like. See the sample survey on pages 40–43 for more ideas.

❑ 1. Fosters a high level of trust among team members.

❑ 2. Acknowledges work and accomplishments with positive reinforcement.

❑ 3. Rewards people for team efforts.

❑ 4. Clarifies the role each individual will play in accomplishing team tasks.

❑ 5. Jointly defines accountability for tasks with key players at the start.

❑ 6. On time for scheduled appointments.

❑ 7. Coaches others in job-related skills as needed.

❑ 8. Assists in setting appropriate targets and goals with two-way discussions.

❑ 9. Gives ongoing performance-related feedback.

❑ 10. Helps to resolve conflicting work priorities.

❑ 11. Helps others to see how their work contributes to the company's success.

❑ 12. Gives people challenges to address rather than mandating changes.

❑ 13. Describes the kind of future s/he would like to see in the organization.

❑ 14. Demonstrates consistent, sustained support for actions that support achieving business plan goals.

❑ 15. Actively supports efforts to meet customer needs.

❑ 16. Inspires people to do their best for the company.

❑ 17. Demonstrates leadership behaviors that support the values of the company.

❑ 18. Tests for alignment with others when it appears that a decision has been made.

❑ 19. Allows experimentation with new approaches to his/her own work.

❑ 20. Demonstrates an awareness of the challenges others face in their work.

❑ 21. Encourages feedback on his/her ability to coach others effectively.

❑ 22. Gives others autonomy to execute work details.

❑ 23. Encourages open discussions among key players when making significant decisions.

Additional leadership characteristics or behaviors you have thought of:

❑ 24. _____

❑ 25. _____

❑ 26. _____

❑ 27. _____

❑ 28. _____

❑ 29. _____

❑ 30. _____

#2: DEVELOPING YOUR OWN SURVEY

A Multipoint Feedback survey is developed to ask specific questions relating to the skills and behaviors associated with your leadership model.

The following are some hints on writing your own Multipoint Feedback survey questions:

I. Brainstorm by yourself or with a group of colleagues, a list of current and future behaviors that you may be expected to demonstrate to be considered successful in your job. Try to think of as many as you can.

> When thinking about various behaviors, remember:
>
> ☞ Behaviors represent those technical, business, and leadership skills that you need in order to do your job most effectively.
>
> ☞ Sometimes organizations have already defined behaviors or competencies for specific jobs. Some positions such as Compensation and Benefits Manager or Sales Account Manager may have a set of behaviors and/or competencies defined by their respective professional organizations.
>
> ☞ Others will assess their perception of your competency level by the actions and behaviors that they actually see you do. Often they will measure this from the perspective of how your actions impact them in their work.

II. Here are some questions to ask yourself:

- "Are each of these really important for me to do well in this job?" Eliminate any that seem extra or irrelevant.

- "Can others observe (see, hear, experience) me demonstrating these competencies?"

- "Can the people I am asking to give me feedback respond to these questions?"

- Ask some colleagues, "Am I missing any additional characteristics that you feel are important?"

- Adjust the wording of each question to fit with the preface statement of, "To what degree does (*insert your name*) . . ."

- Refine the wording of the behaviors described, making sure that each sentence starts with a verb such as *encourages* feedback on your ability to effectively coach others, or *offers* solutions to meet customer needs.

- Make sure you have only single-focus questions, and eliminate compound questions. Including more than one concept in a single question makes it difficult for others to know what to give you feedback on. It also becomes confusing to you when trying to interpret your feedback report.

- You will also need to make choices about the rating scale on your survey. Scales can range from three to twelve intervals. We generally use a 5-point scale because it is simple, yet gives people enough choices to select from. Larger scales tend to get condensed in the interpretation phase and do not really add much value.

- We suggest using approximately 20 to 40 questions to fully define all the aspects of your competency requirements, with each question being different enough from the others that people will believe they are addressing different issues. Too many questions will become tiring and seem redundant for those filling out your survey.

- Review your list of important characteristics, combining, eliminating, and editing to develop a final list.

#2: DEVELOPING
YOUR OWN SURVEY (continued)

III. Here are some important things to think about if you choose to purchase an off-the-shelf survey:

- If you were to score highly on the survey, would this represent a successful profile to you, your boss, and your organization?

- Can you add additional questions you would like feedback on?

- Is the survey worded in language that would be easy for the people with whom you work to understand and respond to?

- Are there a manageable number of questions (between 20 to 40) both for those who will fill them out, and for you to work with the results?

- Do you believe that the people whom you will ask to give you feedback will be able to answer the questions on the survey?

- Do the questions address single-focus areas, and avoid compound questions?

- How does the survey align with your organization's vision of success?

- How will the responses be tallied and presented back to you in a summary report?

- Will there be averages, ranges, and groupings?

- When can you expect to receive the final report?

- Will your scores be compared to national or company-wide average scores?

- What are the costs for individual surveys, reports, and follow-up coaching?

- Will your results be kept confidential?

To help you develop your own Multipoint Feedback Survey, try the following exercise.

EXERCISE: Creating your own questions, pick from the following common list of verbs:

Demonstrate	Help to	Give	Define
Acknowledge	Clarify	Follow	Achieve
Follow-through	Meet	Obtain	Assist
Provide	Experiment	Foster	Recognize
Encourage	Make	Exhibit	Inspire
Accomplish	Involve	Support	Describe

NEVER   SELDOM   ALWAYS

← 1   2   3   4   5 →

To what degree does _____ :
(insert your name)

Here are some sample questions:

1. Foster a high level of trust among team members?
2. Acknowledge the work and accomplishments of others?
3. Clarify the role each individual will play in accomplishing team tasks?
4. Describe the kind of future state she would like to see in her organization?
5. Actively support efforts to meet customer needs?

Try writing your own questions:

6. _____

7. _____

8. _____

9. _____

10. _____

#2: DEVELOPING
YOUR OWN SURVEY (continued)

This is a sample survey designed for our case study.

Pauline Niner chose the following questions and survey for her Multipoint Feedback. See page 29 to review information about Pauline, and some reasons for how her survey was designed.

Multipoint Feedback
Regional Sales Manager

Instructions: Using the scale below, please indicate how well each skill/ behavior listed describes the individual you are rating. The rating you assign should reflect your actual observations and experiences.

Please ✔ *the box that represents your relationship to the individual below:*

❏ **Peer**   ❏ **Direct Report**   ❏ **Manager**   ❏ **Customer**   ❏ **Self**

Accountable for the Success of the Whole Team

Please circle your responses.

Currently, Pauline:	NEVER SELDOM ALWAYS
	1 2 3 4 5
1. Shares best practices so others may adapt.	1 2 3 4 5
2. Sets aside personal goals if they interfere with team success.	1 2 3 4 5
3. Teams with others to better accomplish team objectives.	1 2 3 4 5
4. Openly shares mistakes and failures so others can learn and avoid.	1 2 3 4 5
5. Takes responsibility and ownership for her actions.	1 2 3 4 5

Actively Communicates with Others

Currently, Pauline:

	NEVER	SELDOM		ALWAYS	
	1	2	3	4	5

6. Actively shares her own viewpoints; is a straight-talker. 1 2 3 4 5

7. Ensures clear communications, frames every conversation. 1 2 3 4 5

8. Keeps others informed about business issues affecting them. 1 2 3 4 5

9. Listens to the needs and viewpoints of others even if different from her own. 1 2 3 4 5

10. Asks for and accepts feedback from peers in a positive manner. 1 2 3 4 5

Collaborative and Dependable

Currently, Pauline:

11. Adheres to team rules of conduct and norms. 1 2 3 4 5

12. Actively aligns work and people to achieve business objectives. 1 2 3 4 5

13. Follows through on commitments, keeps her promises. 1 2 3 4 5

14. Demonstrates a willingness to learn new skills and unlearn outdated ways. 1 2 3 4 5

15. Trusts others and can be trusted herself. 1 2 3 4 5

#2: DEVELOPING YOUR OWN SURVEY (continued)

Motivates Others to Align for Success

Currently, Pauline:

		NEVER	SELDOM		ALWAYS
		1	2	3	4	5
16.	Projects a positive attitude; imparts enthusiasm.	1	2	3	4	5
17.	Acknowledges the contributions of others.	1	2	3	4	5
18.	Brings information and insights to help solve problems and make decisions.	1	2	3	4	5
19.	Takes initiative without waiting to be asked.	1	2	3	4	5
20.	Seeks the input of other team members to build strategies and action plans.	1	2	3	4	5

Additional Upward Feedback Questions (to be completed by direct reports only).

Currently, Pauline:

21.	Acknowledges your work and accomplishments with positive reinforcement.	1	2	3	4	5
22.	Rewards you for your team efforts.	1	2	3	4	5
23.	Clarifies the role each individual will play in accomplishing team tasks.	1	2	3	4	5
24.	Coaches you in job-related skills as needed.	1	2	3	4	5
25.	Assists you in setting appropriate targets and goals through meaningful dialogue.	1	2	3	4	5
26.	Gives you ongoing performance-related feedback.	1	2	3	4	5
27.	Describes the kind of future state she would like to see in your organization.	1	2	3	4	5

	NEVER	SELDOM	ALWAYS
	1 2 3 4 5		

28. Actively supports your efforts to meet customer needs.   1 2 3 4 5

29. Experiments with new approaches in her own work.   1 2 3 4 5

30. Gives you autonomy to execute work details.   1 2 3 4 5

Multipoint Feedback Comments

Please ✔ the box that represents your relationship to the individual below:

❏ **Peer**   ❏ **Direct Report**   ❏ **Manager**   ❏ **Customer**   ❏ **Self**

Currently, I most value from Pauline:
Currently, I would like Pauline to work on:
I would like to see more of:
I would like to see less of:

3: CHOOSING YOUR FEEDBACK TEAM

Direct Report Selection for Upward Feedback

We recommend that you invite all of your direct reports to participate in your Upward Feedback. Selecting only a few sends a message that you really only want to hear from certain individuals and not others. Your job is to request and act upon the feedback you receive. Some individuals will naturally self-select themselves out of the process by not returning the feedback survey. Let them do so, but at least give them the opportunity to withdraw.

Consider these issues:

▶ If there are sub-teams within your team of direct reports who may experience your leadership in very different ways based on the type of interaction you have with them (such as, various geographical locations or different reporting structure expectations), it may make sense to break your feedback data into two discrete sets so you can better understand the data. Be sure to set this up at the start so the surveys can be coded and participants informed of your intent to sort responses.

▶ Individuals on your team who have worked for you less than four months may not be able to adequately answer the feedback survey. Depending on the situation, you may want to give them the option to respond, or ask that they not fill out a survey (because of being new), but definitely have them participate in the team feedback meeting.

▶ In order to maintain the anonymity of the feedback providers, at least four direct reports should be asked to respond to the survey with at least three actually turning in responses. Your report should indicate how many people actually turned them in, as well as how many were asked to participate (N = 8/12 where the N means number in statistical terms. In this case, 12 were invited and 8 actually responded).

Peer and Customer Selection

▶ It is important with this process to ask for feedback from at least five peers and five customers who are qualified (you would value their feedback) and able (opportunity to observe firsthand) to give feedback.

▶ If you are part of a work team, you will want to ask for feedback from each of the other members of your team. It is wise to ask them all to contribute so it does not appear that you only want feedback from certain people. They will opt out if for any reason they do not feel comfortable participating.

▶ Select internal customers who work "downstream" from you. These are the people who receive the work (products and/or services) that you produce. Maintaining and improving working relationships between customers and suppliers (you are the supplier in this case) will improve overall organizational effectiveness.

▶ Remember, questions asked on the survey must be relevant to the observable areas which your peers or customers can provide feedback on.

Develop a list of the direct reports, peers, and customers you would like feedback from:

UPWARD	PEER	CUSTOMERS

#4: HOLDING A KICK-OFF MEETING

▶ Schedule a 45 to 60 minute kick-off meeting with your direct reports. This topic could be folded into the agenda of another meeting or held separately. Send a note, voice-mail, e-mail message, or stop by and invite your peers and customers to participate. Give them the survey and cover letter with very specific information about what you would like them to do. Assure them that you value and appreciate them taking the time to give you some feedback.

▶ In the beginning, it is really important to have clear communication about why you are doing Multipoint Feedback, what others will be asked to do, and what you intend to do with the results.

▶ Employees new to the Multipoint Feedback process are often concerned about providing feedback, fearing that if they are truly open and honest, there could be hurt feelings or negative consequences from their supervisor or peers. This is especially true in an organization where the overall level of trust is low. It is important to reassure people throughout this process that you are very interested in hearing from them, that you will value their feedback, and that there will be no negative consequences associated with their participation.

▶ We have seen a significantly higher level of participation in returning surveys when there is a personal invitation extended by the requesting manager rather than simply mailing out the surveys unannounced.

Most direct reports are fairly comfortable providing feedback when:

1. Their input is anonymous (no names or codes on the surveys).

2. Surveys are routed to a neutral third party and collated into a summary report.

3. Written comments are restated and combined, rather than shared as direct quotes.

4. They trust that there will not be negative consequences for their manager, which could result in retaliation against them.

Checklist for Planning Your Kick-Off Meeting

❏   Prepare an introduction describing why you are doing a Multipoint Feedback process, what you hope to gain, and specifically, what you will need from the participants.

❏   Develop a timeline for survey distribution and return, report preparation, receiving your feedback report, and sharing the final results with them.

❏   Describe clearly what you expect: open and honest feedback, specific examples in the comment section, and turning the survey in on time.

❏   Clarify your agreement: input will be treated as anonymous, your results will be confidential, and you will share a summary of the feedback (not necessarily the actual feedback report) with all participants.

❏   Distribute surveys and cover letters to each person.

❏   Express your appreciation for their time and willingness to give you honest feedback.

Read on for a sample of Pauline's Kick-Off Meeting agenda.

#4: HOLDING A KICK-OFF MEETING (continued)

To: Product ZQW Sales Team

From: Pauline Niner   March 1, 1997

Re: Kick-Off Meeting for my Multipoint Feedback

We have scheduled a Kick-Off Meeting on March 13th, from 8:00 A.M.–9:00 A.M. in Conference Room D. I would really appreciate your attendance. The agenda is as follows:

8:00   Background and overview of the Multipoint Feedback process.

          My timeline, hopes, and expectations for going forward.

          My agreements with you for handling the feedback and follow-up.

8:30   Distribute surveys and cover letters.

          Questions and answers.

9:00   Appreciation and closing.

P A R T

V

The Feedback Loop

#5: SURVEY DISTRIBUTION

Multipoint Feedback surveys can either be mailed or handed out to each participant with an attached cover letter. The cover letter restates the subjects addressed during the Kick-Off Meeting.

We recommend you have the surveys returned to a neutral third party within or outside of your organization. This often helps people believe that their individual feedback will be treated anonymously and increases the likelihood that the results will be tabulated in a fair and objective manner.

Surveys can be returned in one of three ways:

1. Completed during a meeting and turned in directly (+ high return rates; – increased pressure on participants for filling surveys out)

2. Faxed to third party (+ quick return and participant retains their copy; – some fax machines include a name, so a third party may be able to identify the source)

3. Mail back (+ allows for time to complete and total anonymity; – more costly, time consuming, and slower/lower return rates)

Remember: To get the best return rate, it is helpful to give people two weeks between the date you distribute the feedback surveys to the date you are requesting the surveys be returned.

Example: Surveys distributed on: March 15th

Surveys returned by: March 31st

The example on the following page shows Pauline's cover letter.

#5: SURVEY DISTRIBUTION (continued)

To: Product ZQW Sales Team

From: Pauline Niner   March 13, 1997

Re: Multipoint Feedback

I am sending you this survey with the hope of receiving feedback on my effectiveness in working with you. I would appreciate your taking the time to complete the following Multipoint Feedback Survey. The survey provides you with a framework to discuss your satisfactions as well as your concerns. Please be as specific as possible and give examples whenever you can.

An objective third party will compile my feedback report. Your responses are treated anonymously and I will receive an average score with ranges for each question. Comments will be grouped into common themes rather than restated as direct quotes. You may leave questions blank if you feel that you are unable to answer. Please print clearly in ink and fax your completed surveys to (510) 555-1234 no later than March 31st. I will receive my summary feedback in early July and would like to meet with you later in the month to share the highlights with you. At that time I will ask for clarification (if needed) and suggestions for going forward. If you have further questions, please call me, or call The York Consulting Team at (510) 555-1233.

#6: SURVEY RETURN AND REPORT PREPARATION

Here are some options to consider when creating your report format (which must be planned before you launch).

1. There are a number of alternatives for tallying and displaying numerical responses in your Multipoint Feedback report. The easiest and most common method is to display the average score for each question by respondent group. To compute the average score, add up individual scores and divide by the number of responses:

$$3.5 + 4.0 + 2.5 + 2.0 = 12.0$$

$$12 \text{ divided by } 4 = 3.0$$

Averages give you a quick overall summary to sort out your strengths (highest scores) and opportunity areas (lowest scores). If your objective is to quickly identify key strengths to leverage and significant opportunities to improve, then average scores work quite well. The downside to averages is that you can not tell if everyone scored you the same. In the above case, it could have been all 3.0s, or if some scored you really high and others really low, $5.0 + 5.0 - 1.0 + 1.0$ also equals 12 with an average score of 3.0. Including both the average scores and the range or distribution of scores gives you the most information.

2. When you receive input from several different groups—direct reports, peers, customers, yourself, and your manager—you will want to see your scores for each group as well as overall combined scores. These can be displayed as averages or graphical comparisons to help you see if your strengths differ from different perspectives. Visual graphics are helpful to understanding contrasts and differences among groups.

3. Some people may have subsets within respondent groups, such as ten direct reports who work in the southern office and seven who work in the northern office. Be sure to discuss this ahead of time so that the surveys can be coded and survey results grouped accordingly. As a rule of thumb, each subgroup should have at least four to five members to preserve anonymity.

4. Comments can be synthesized or combined together to reflect the viewpoints of the participants. Direct quotes can easily be traced to individuals since they are usually written in language and wording unique to each person. Comments should also be sorted and displayed by respondent groups. Often people are reluctant to write comments for fear of loosing their anonymity. We have found that people tend to write more the second round of Multipoint Feedback once they feel comfortable with the process. Comments are often very helpful in making sense of the numerical averages.

Multipoint Feedback Sample Summary Report
Pauline Niner: March 1997

Of 30 Feedback Surveys sent out requesting input, 21 were completed and returned	Overall 21/30	Direct Reports 8/10	Peers 7/11	Customer 5/8	Manager 1/1	Self 1/1
Accountable for the Success of the Whole Team						
1. Shares best practices so others may adapt.	3.35	2.70	3.60	3.10	4.00	4.00
2. Sets aside personal goals if they interfere with team success.	2.75	2.50	3.20	2.80	3.00	3.00
3. Teams with others to better accomplish team objectives.	3.50	3.00	3.60	3.00	4.00	4.00
4. Openly shares mistakes and failures so others can learn and avoid.	3.40	3.80	4.00	3.20	3.00	3.00
5. Takes responsibility and ownership for her actions.	2.70	240	3.00	2.80	3.00	3.00
Category Average	**3.02**	**2.55**	**3.30**	**2.95**	**3.50**	**3.50**
Actively Communicates with Others						
6. Actively shares her own viewpoints, is a straight-talker.	4.50	4.00	4.60	4.80	5.00	5.00
7. Ensures clear communications; frames every conversation.	3.60	3.20	3.40	3.20	4.00	4.00
8. Keeps others informed about business issues affecting them.	3.40	2.80	3.20	4.00	4.00	4.00
9. Listens to the needs and viewpoints of others even if different from her own.	2.80	2.60	2.80	3.80	3.00	3.00

10. Asks for and accepts feedback from peers in a positive manner.	4.00	4.00	3.60	3.80	3.40	3.70
Category Average	**4.50**	**4.50**	**4.20**	**4.20**	**3.70**	**4.10**
Collaborative and Dependable						
11. Adheres to team rules of conduct and norms.	3.00	3.00	4.00	3.60	3.40	3.20
12. Actively aligns work and people to achieve business objectives.	3.00	4.00	3.60	3.80	3.00	3.50
13. Follows through on commitments, keeps her promises.	3.00	3.00	4.60	2.80	3.20	3.10
14. Demonstrates a willingness to learn new skills and unlearn outdated ways.	4.00	3.00	4.80	3.00	2.60	2.80
15. Trusts others and can be trusted herself.	3.00	4.00	4.60	3.00	2.20	3.10
Category Average	**3.00**	**3.50**	**4.30**	**3.30**	**2.80**	**3.15**
Motivates Others to Align for Success						
16. Projects a positive attitude; imparts enthusiasm.	5.00	5.00	5.00	4.60	4.00	4.50
17. Acknowledges the contributions of others.	4.00	5.00	4.80	4.20	3.80	4.40
18. Brings information and insights to help solve problems and make decisions.	5.00	5.00	4.80	4.40	3.20	4.10
19. Takes initiative without waiting to be asked.	4.00	4.00	5.00	4.60	4.40	4.20
20. Seeks the input of other team members to build strategies and action plans.	4.00	4.00	4.60	3.20	2.40	3.20
Category Average	**4.50**	**4.50**	**4.80**	**3.90**	**3.20**	**3.85**

Multipoint Feedback Sample Summary Report (continued)
Pauline Niner: March 1997

	Overall 21/30	Direct Reports 8/10	Peers 7/11	Customer 5/8	Manager 1/1	Self 1/1
Upward Feedback (Received from direct reports only)						
21. Acknowledges your work and accomplishments with positive reinforcements.		3.80				3.00
22. Rewards you for your team efforts.		3.20				3.00
23. Clarifies the role each individual will play in accomplishing team tasks.		3.20				3.00
24. Coaches you in job-related skills as needed.		3.60				4.00
25. Assists you in setting appropriate targets and goals through meaningful dialogue.		3.20				3.00
26. Gives you ongoing performance-related feedback.		2.80				3.00
27. Describes the kind of future state she would like to see in your organization.		3.60				3.00
28. Actively supports your efforts to meet customer needs.		4.00				4.00
29. Experiments with new approaches in her own work.		3.20				3.00
30. Gives you autonomy to execute work details.		4.60				3.00
Category Average		**3.52**				**3.20**

Pauline Niner: Sample Narrative Summary

D = Direct Report;   P = Peer;   C = Customer;   M = Manager Comments

(BUILDING SYNERGY AND TEAMWORK)

Strengths:

- You bring a lot of good ideas to our team, you are creative and tend to "think out-of-the-box." **(D)**

- You take the time to acknowledge the good work we do; others comment to us that you have shared something positive about our work with them. **(D)**

Opportunity Areas:

- We need more interaction about what is going on in our region and what will be needed in the future. We hear a lot of rumors and do not get enough information to feel clear and comfortable. **(D)**

- We would like to better understand our role when you assign new tasks. We seem to be confused and tripping over each other at times. **(D)**

- We would like to be involved earlier on in the planning process. At times it does not seem that you really want our input because the decisions have already been made. **(P)**

(BUILDING INDIVIDUAL CAPABILITY)

Strengths:

- You suggest training programs that might be helpful to us. You take the time to answer questions when we meet one-to-one with you. **(D)**

- You are fair with performance appraisals. **(D)**

PAULINE NINER: SAMPLE NARRATIVE SUMMARY (continued)

Opportunity Areas:

- You could become more knowledgeable about the job requirements of the people who report to you. It gets confusing as to who to go to. **(P)**

- You need to give us more ongoing performance feedback. We have no idea where we stand with you overall. Although you give specific feedback close to events, it is difficult to add these up. **(D)**

- Sometimes your feedback feels quite punitive, especially when it is given in front of others. **(D)**

- We respect your thoughts and expertise and would appreciate more constructive feedback from you on an ongoing basis. **(P)**

LEADING AND BUILDING SHARED VISION

Strengths:

- You are very creative and future focused. **(C)**

- You try to share your vision of the future with us and you schedule quarterly Sales Manager meetings to keep us informed. **(C)**

Opportunity Areas:

- We would appreciate it if you could spend more time with us discussing your thoughts about the future of our business. **(D)**

- Sometimes we do not feel like we have the opportunity to be part of your vision, it feels like it is yours alone. **(D)**

#7: REVIEWING YOUR FEEDBACK

The following are some key points to remember when you start interpreting the results of your Multipoint Feedback Report.

► Your feedback from others represents their perceptions. You may not agree, or believe they are wrong; however, try to listen to what they are saying so that you can learn. Their perceptions are real to them (and very helpful for you to know).

► This information is not new; it existed in the perceptions others held of you before you began your Multipoint Feedback process. It only looks more real because it now includes written feedback from several individuals combined into a report.

► Often you will get feedback that seems to be inconsistent between groups or even within the same group. Some individuals will see areas as strengths while others see them as opportunities. Sometimes we interact differently with different groups of people. A customer might say that you "listen well and are always open to my needs," while a peer may feel that you "never listen." Both are true and can easily represent different perspectives from different people.

► It is more important to identify a few key themes to work on rather than to develop a long list of many areas to improve. If you pick the strongest overall opportunities to work on, often many of the smaller ones will get better as well.

► Everyone has both strengths and opportunity areas. Rejoice in both! Feedback from others is a gift that helps build strong relationships and performance. Look for ways to use your strengths to improve your opportunity areas.

► Simple reports pointing to key strength and opportunity areas will be more meaningful and easier to act upon than lengthy, complex volumes. Avoid complicated reports loaded with multiple views of your results and extensive data, or you may drown in "analysis-paralysis."

HOW TO INTERPRET YOUR FEEDBACK REPORT

(This may be done with a third-party coach. Guidelines for working through this step together follow in the upcoming pages.)

1. Read through your summary report first to get an overview of what is included in the report. Make sure that you understand how the report was put together, so you know what you are looking at. For example:

- How many people actually gave you feedback? This number may be different from the actual number of people whom you asked for feedback. In some cases, you may see some variation by question if people chose not to respond to certain questions.

- Are you looking at average scores (the total scores added together divided by the number of people giving feedback), or number of responses distributed in categories on a scale? Average scores will give you a blend of the highs and lows; distributed scores will show you the range or variations in the individual scores.

- Be sure you understand how the scores are reflected from each subgroup. Your boss, direct reports, peers, customers, and self will probably have a separate listing. Sometimes you may see them all added together to give you an overall picture.

2. Look at comparisons between how you scored yourself and how others scored you for each question. If this is your first time doing a Multipoint Feedback process, you may find that your self scores are quite a bit higher or lower than the other groupings. In time, you will become more accurate in understanding how others see your strengths and opportunity areas. Look for gaps of at least one full point or greater, and list the top five largest gaps in the following table. Smaller gaps are probably not worth attending to for now. Note in the "Their Score" column whether this gap is an Upward, Peer, Boss, or Customer feedback score.

Comparisons between self scores and scores from others:

QUESTIONS	MY SCORE	THEIR SCORE	GAP
1.			
2.			
3.			
4.			
5.			

3. Next look for key *strengths* and *opportunity areas* in your feedback from others. Fill in the following charts. Pick the top and bottom three to five scores from each feedback group.

Upward Feedback

TOP STRENGTHS	TOP OPPORTUNITY AREAS

Peer Feedback

TOP STRENGTHS	TOP OPPORTUNITY AREAS

HOW TO INTERPRET YOUR FEEDBACK REPORT (continued)

Manager Feedback

TOP STRENGTHS	TOP OPPORTUNITY AREAS

Customer Feedback

TOP STRENGTHS	TOP OPPORTUNITY AREAS

4. Next, carefully look over your key strengths and opportunity area scores to understand any consistent themes. Using the following table, write some summary statements for yourself to describe overall strengths and opportunity themes from each feedback group.

Upward Feedback

Others see my strengths as being able to:	Others see me as having some opportunity areas in:

Peer Feedback

Others see my strengths as being able to:	Others see me as having some opportunity areas in:

HOW TO INTERPRET YOUR FEEDBACK REPORT (continued)

Manager Feedback

My manager sees my strengths as being able to:	My manager sees me as having some opportunity areas in:

Customer Feedback

Others see my strengths as being able to:	Others see me as having some opportunity areas in:

5. Now look for themes or inconsistencies between each feedback group. Are there some overall strength and opportunity areas where you see big differences?

Overall Themes	Inconsistencies Between Feedback Groups

6. Sometimes the feedback will be very familiar to you, "you've heard it before," and other times certain points may come as a real surprise. In the following table, note your Familiar Feedback and Surprises.

Familiar Feedback	Surprises

If you are using a third-party coach to assist you and your team with the Multipoint Process, it will be helpful for them to review your feedback report with you. Analyzing your feedback report using the above framework will assist you in thinking through the items you would like to receive more specific information on during your team feedback meeting. Keep the following agenda in mind when planning for your initial feedback meeting.

HOW TO INTERPRET YOUR FEEDBACK REPORT (continued)

Discuss the following with your coach during your individual feedback session:

- Review meeting agenda, roles, norms, and time commitments for the session.

- Share self-assessment results and discuss questions that are a high priority for you. Some questions may reflect particular areas you have already been working on, others may seem less important at this time.

- Data Review: Review each category, highlighting high and low scores indicating your top three to five strengths and opportunity areas.

- Identify themes: discuss some summary themes to describe what the overall feedback is telling you.

- Comparisons: Note the similarities and gaps between your self-assessment and between respondent groups.

- Surprises: Note areas that surprise you and try to imagine why people might feel this way.

- Draw on strengths: How can you use your strengths to develop your opportunity areas?

- Brainstorm development approaches: Discuss where you would ideally like your scores to be and identifying options for how you might get there.

- Share with your boss: Discuss this as an option, what are the potential risks or gains? In what form would you share your results, and what would you hope to gain from this?

- Share with your direct reports: designing a team feedback meeting agenda to highlight the top three to five Strengths and top three to five Opportunity Areas (approximate numbers that seem to work well). In planning for your Team Feedback Meeting, you may want to review the chart on the following page to determine how ready your team may be for this type of discussion. If your team is at the far left side, they may not have developed the skills needed to maintain an open and candid feedback discussion. In this case you will want to utilize an experienced facilitator to assist you. However, if your team is on the far right side and your scores look pretty good, you may be comfortable going ahead on your own. Some people accidentally jump into a Multipoint Team Feedback meeting with a team who have not yet developed the experience or skills to function at this level.

- Critique the process with those involved, and close the meeting.

Team Meeting Developmental Process

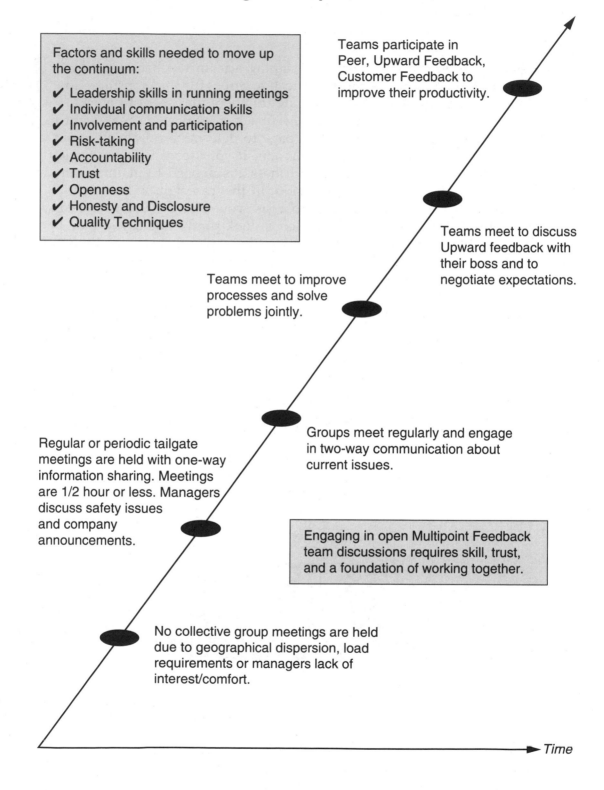

Factors and skills needed to move up the continuum:

✔ Leadership skills in running meetings
✔ Individual communication skills
✔ Involvement and participation
✔ Risk-taking
✔ Accountability
✔ Trust
✔ Openness
✔ Honesty and Disclosure
✔ Quality Techniques

Teams participate in Peer, Upward Feedback, Customer Feedback to improve their productivity.

Teams meet to discuss Upward feedback with their boss and to negotiate expectations.

Teams meet to improve processes and solve problems jointly.

Groups meet regularly and engage in two-way communication about current issues.

Regular or periodic tailgate meetings are held with one-way information sharing. Meetings are 1/2 hour or less. Managers discuss safety issues and company announcements.

Engaging in open Multipoint Feedback team discussions requires skill, trust, and a foundation of working together.

No collective group meetings are held due to geographical dispersion, load requirements or managers lack of interest/comfort.

Time

The chart below helps to clarify roles for Individual Feedback Meetings with a third-party coach.

THIRD-PARTY COACH	MANAGER
Asking Questions	Self-Exploring
Expanding Options	Alternative Selecting
Process Facilitator	Content Expert
Co-Navigator	Co-Navigator
Coach	Central Player
Reflecting the Feedback	Understanding the Data
Support and Encouragement	Learning and Development

Meeting Norms

Confidentiality and Sensitivity

Mutual Trust and Understanding

Facilitation and Learning

Openness and Honesty

#8: HOLDING YOUR TEAM FEEDBACK MEETING

When preparing for your team meeting consider:

Prior to the Meeting:

- Plan to allow a minimum of two hours for this meeting. It is fine to build this into your regular meeting agenda or use it as a stand-alone meeting topic. Any less than two hours does not give enough time to set the stage, build trust and confidence in the process, and enable people to engage in an open, honest, and focused discussion. Trust us on this one!

- The Team Feedback Meeting with your direct reports is one of the most critical steps in the Multipoint Feedback process. Although your summary report will give you some highlights about where you show strengths and opportunities for improvement, it is in the feedback meeting where the real action occurs. One of the biggest and costliest errors managers make is to take the feedback and go off by themselves to figure out what to do about it. You are likely to invest in changes that are more cumbersome and less effective than the specific suggestions your team will give you. Pick the top areas and ask them to brainstorm suggestions. They will most likely give you specific and concrete next steps. In addition, the more you share and discuss this with them, the more they will want to support your changes. They will probably even agree to do things to help you be more successful! You will have a much better chance of showing improvement on your next round if you worked on the areas that were important to them. Many managers have immersed themselves in training following Multipoint Feedback only to find no improvement or decreasing scores the next time around. Get close to your people to find out what success really would look like from their eyes.

- Invite your entire direct report team to the meeting. Encourage everyone to come. If a number of them are not able to attend, reschedule the meeting to a more convenient time.

- You will need a private meeting room set up for a discussion with chairs in a semicircle or around a large table. Plan to have a flip chart (paper and a stand), magic markers, tape, and wall space for hanging papers.

- These meetings tend to be most successful when you send out an agenda confirming logistics, meeting objectives, and discussion topics.

During the Meeting:

- Review the agenda, meeting norms, and outcomes. Post them on the wall. Explain your role and that of any others who may be helping you during the meeting. Reassure them that the feedback they gave on the surveys was anonymous and that it is not your intent to try to figure out who said what.

- Thank them for acknowledging specific strengths and/or acknowledge that these areas are important to you and in fact you have been working on them.

- Take about 15 to 20 minutes to discuss your top three to five strengths. Even though this may feel uncomfortable to you, you don't want to inadvertently stop doing things that they appreciate. It is also a good opportunity for the members of your team to hear the discussion on specific behaviors and strengths for their own benefit. You'll find that they start changing their own behaviors when they get a clear picture of what others value.

> Ask them to tell you what it is that they see you do that leads them to see these behaviors as strengths and for suggestions on how you could become even stronger.

#8: HOLDING YOUR TEAM FEEDBACK MEETING (continued)

- Share your top three to five opportunity areas. These may be your lowest scores, or scores that represent significant gaps either between your self-assessment and their scores, or areas that you feel are critical and you would like to see your scores to be higher.

  ► Take the opportunities one at a time, and for each one ask participants to spend five to seven minutes brainstorming:

  > "What would it look like to you if this were to become a strength rather than an opportunity area (or weakness, or low score) for me? What specific things would I do or not do?"

  ► On a flip chart record and post their responses, asking for clarification or for some examples. (Do not evaluate their ideas or give any feedback at this point.)

  ► Complete all three to five opportunities in the same manner. Then, stand back and look at their ideas. Try to accept them and understand the issues from their point of view. Work hard to avoid getting defensive, the minute you start getting defensive; angry or stop listening, it will likely shut down their willingness to be open and give you honest suggestions. Also avoid explaining, rationalizing, and rehashing past events. Learn from them and go on. Do not try to single out individuals with "Who said this?" or "How many of you feel this way?" People will not be honest, and they will not tattle on each other. Take lots of notes, this will help you keep from being defensive and buy you some time to think about it later when you are not under pressure. For each area, pick the things that you are most willing and able to do. Give a brief explanation as to why you can not do the others, and ask for support going forward from them. This will most likely include your working on the issues and the team giving you ongoing feedback and reinforcement.

  ► Tell them that they can expect a follow-up Multipoint Feedback Survey in nine to twelve months.

  ► Thank them for their willingness to participate, and for their helpful suggestions.

Sample Team Feedback Meeting Agenda for Pauline

PURPOSE

- Acknowledgment and appreciation for feedback

- Gain clarification as to what behaviors led to strengths and opportunity areas

- Jointly negotiate a path forward for behavior change and improvement

AGENDA

Welcome—Appreciation

- Overview of Purpose and Meeting Agenda

- Meeting Norms and Assumptions

Helpful Meeting Norms (post on wall):

☆ *Honesty and openness is encouraged.*

☆ *Confidentiality is appreciated.*

☆ *Listening is critical.*

☆ *Sensitivity and caring will make this easier for all of us.*

☆ *We need to trust and help each other through this process.*

☆ *Your presence and full attention is needed by the team.*

Sample Team Feedback Meeting Agenda for Pauline *(continued)*

Assumptions (discuss these during your introduction):

- Change is most successful when we have a clear picture of specifically what the change should look like.

- We can be most productive if we focus on the future together and learn from the past.

- We are in the midst of major changes. This requires a willingness to be vulnerable and to change personal behaviors. Although previous behaviors were role modeled, accepted, and reinforced, we know that we need to be different in the future. The rules of the game have changed and I recognize that I am on a learning curve.

- All feedback from you has been anonymous. Although some of you may recognize your comments, no one but you knows the comment came from you. It is not my intent to try to figure out who said what but rather to look forward and learn what needs to change. (Use this only if you are sharing narrative comments with them.)

Key strengths: "What does it look like, specifically, when I'm doing this well?"

- Acknowledging work you do
- Actively supporting your efforts to meet customer needs
- Sharing important information

Key Opportunity Areas: "What would it look like, going forward, if I were doing this really well?" or "What would it take to turn this from an opportunity area into a future strength?"

- Building trust with the people I work with
- Coaching in job-related skills
- Ensuring clear communication

Closing: Next steps, commitments, and thank you.

- Follow-up with peers, customers, and supervisor. Although you may not wish to conduct a follow-up meeting with everyone who gave you input (the direct report group is the most important for this step) we encourage a written response to others. Your primary purpose in sending the follow-up letter is to thank them and encourage them to continue to give you feedback. Their perceptions are out there at all times, you might as well know about them so you can do something if needed. Review the following to see how Pauline handled a follow-up letter to her peers.

SAMPLE FOLLOW-UP LETTER

To: Fellow Regional Sales Managers

From: Pauline Niner   April 15, 1997

I want to personally thank each of you for the time you took to complete my Multipoint Feedback surveys. I appreciate your willingness to provide written comments as well as the numerical scores.

Based on the feedback, I understand my key strengths to be:

- Contributing suggestions in peer team meetings

- Responding to customer needs, and building proactive sales approaches.

- Being available to discuss issues that concern others.

The opportunity areas that I heard and intend to focus on in the coming months are:

- Following through on commitments I make to each of you.

- Being on time for appointments.

- Alerting you to challenges going on in my own team.

I encourage you to continue to let me know about the things that you feel I do that are value-added as well as those that I could do differently to further our team performance. Only through your ongoing support will I grow as a manager and contributor.

Thanks again for your input,

Pauline

P A R T

VI

Completing the Process

#9: DEVELOPING AN ACTION PLAN

After you have completed the previous steps you are ready to put it all together and develop an action plan for yourself. Develop your action plan to address the feedback received during the team feedback meeting, your summary report, and any insights you may have received from others. We encourage you to share this part with your manager in order to gain his or her support during the development phase. Look through the following plan to see how Pauline plans to address her development areas.

Pauline's Developmental Action Plan

Development Goal: Improve leadership with my team so we can achieve greater team sales results.

Development Areas	. . . I'll Know I've Succeeded When . . .	. . . The Activities Which Will Help Me Develop Each Area Include:	. . . Resources I Can Use . . .	. . . My First Step in Each Area Will Be . . .	. . . Deadlines To Shoot For Are . . .
Build Trust with My Team		• Give Positive Feedback • Don't Criticize in Front of Others • Seek their Input	• Get Coaching • Set Off-site Meeting	Give each person positive feedback	1st Step _____ 12/8 Completion 12/8
Ensuring Clear Communication		• Ask for Feedback • Test for Understanding • Listen More—Talk Less	• My Team	Ask for feedback at the end of the next staff meeting	1st Step _____ 12/13 Completion 12/13
Coaching Others		• Practice • Schedule Time • Be Spontaneous	• Crisp Book on Coaching • Ask Nancy to Mentor Me	Set up first appointment	1st Step _____ 12/31 Completion 12/31
Follow Through with Commitments		• Write Things Down • Build in Planning Time • Say 'No' if I Really Can't Deliver	• Day Planner	Buy a Day Planner	1st Step _____ 12/15 Completion 12/15

#10: NEXT STEPS AND FOLLOW-UP

Follow-Up Coaching

Experienced management coaches can provide specific suggestions for continuous improvement, as well as helpful models and tools to explain new ways of working. They may be able to recommend training and other developmental options and share their personal observations to help you in understanding how to apply your current strengths to work on your opportunity development areas.

Check-In Cards

Once you commit to action steps as a result of the Multipoint Feedback process, many managers find it helpful to send out follow-up Check-In Cards. The cards are mailed to your original feedback team (direct reports, peers, customers, and boss) at a designated interval (generally four to six months) so they can provide encouragement, suggestions, and to remind them of the commitments made.

Action (using the attached form)

- Write your name on the "Manager's Name" line item.

- Enter the three areas you have been working on as a result of Multipoint Feedback.

- Enter a return date on the "By" line item (give participants two weeks).

- Enter your return address.

- Photocopy the Check-In Sheet and distribute to team members.

- Let your team know that you are utilizing Check-In Cards as a follow-up coaching tool to the feedback you received during Multipoint Feedback. Encourage team members to respond to the Check-In Cards, as their feedback is critical in helping to reinforce behavior changes you are trying to make.

NEXT STEPS AND FOLLOW-UP (continued)

Sample Multipoint Feedback
Check-In Card

Your Name _____

Purpose: To receive feedback and reinforcement on the behavior changes being made as a result of my initial round of Multipoint Feedback (enter date you initiated process).

Key Opportunity Areas I have been working on include: (fill in line items below.)

1. _____

2. _____

3. _____

Below, please provide me with specific feedback on the opportunity areas described:

In what ways have I been effective and/or made improvements?

In what ways am I still performing old behaviors which could be improved?

Any suggestions for future development?

Please return to: (Give your address)   By: (Enter the due date)

Thank you for taking the time to respond!

Subsequent Rounds

Multipoint Feedback is most effective when used as an ongoing process versus a single event. We advise waiting at least six months and no more than 18 months between rounds of feedback. With each subsequent round, ask that previous scores be included for comparison, upgrade your survey to make sure it addresses any specific areas that were mentioned often in the comments, and include a Changes Since Last Feedback comment page when sending out your surveys to highlight improving areas and continuing concerns.

Changes Since Last Feedback

Continuing strengths:

Prior concerns that have improved:

Continuing concerns:

Comments:

P A R T

VII

Test Your Learning

MULTIPOINT FEEDBACK CROSSWORD PUZZLE

You are now ready to start your own Multipoint Feedback. Test your learning with the following crossword puzzle. Answers are on page 88.

Full Circle Feedback

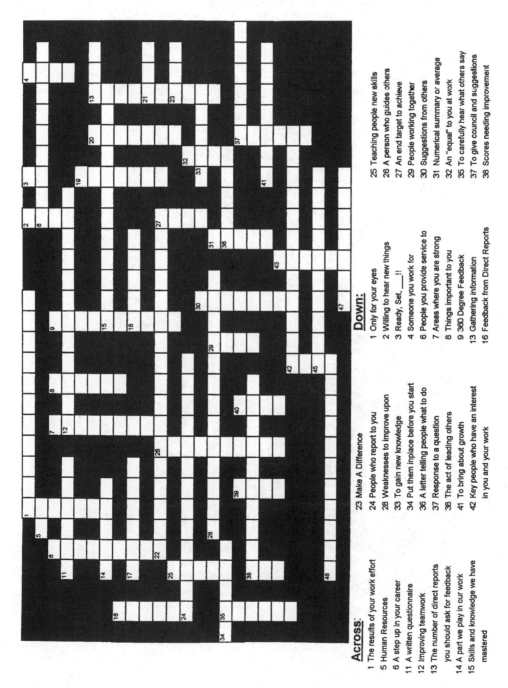

Across:

1 The results of your work effort
5 Human Resources
6 A step up in your career
11 A written questionnaire
12 Improving teamwork
13 The number of direct reports you should ask for feedback
14 A part we play in our work
15 Skills and knowledge we have mastered
23 Make A Difference
24 People who report to you
28 Weaknesses to improve upon
33 To gain new knowledge
34 Put them inplace before you start
36 A letter telling people what to do
37 Response to a question
38 The act of leading others
41 To bring about growth
42 Key people who have an interest in you and your work

Down:

1 Only for your eyes
2 Willing to hear new things
3 Ready, Set, ___!!
4 Someone you work for
6 People you provide service to
7 Areas where you are strong
8 Things important to you
9 360 Degree Feedback
13 Gathering information
16 Feedback from Direct Reports
25 Teaching people new skills
26 A person who guides others
27 An end target to achieve
29 People working together
30 Suggestions from others
31 Numerical summary or average
32 An "equal" to you at work
35 To carefully hear what others say
37 To give council and suggestions
38 Scores needing improvement

Full Circle Feedback

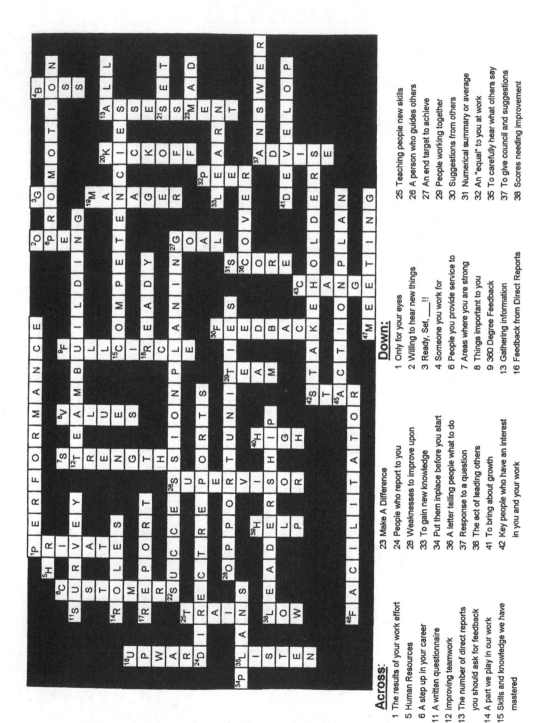

Across:

1 The results of your work effort
5 Human Resources
6 A step up in your career
11 A written questionnaire
12 Improving teamwork
13 The number of direct reports you should ask for feedback
14 A part we play in our work
15 Skills and knowledge we have mastered
23 Make A Difference
24 People who report to you
28 Weaknesses to improve upon
33 To gain new knowledge
34 Put them inplace before you start
36 A letter telling people what to do
37 Response to a question
38 The act of leading others
41 To bring about growth
42 Key people who have an interest in you and your work

Down:

1 Only for your eyes
2 Willing to hear new things
3 Ready, Set, ___!!
4 Someone you work for
6 People you provide service to
7 Areas where you are strong
8 Things important to you
9 360 Degree Feedback
13 Gathering information
16 Feedback from Direct Reports
25 Teaching people new skills
26 A person who guides others
27 An end target to achieve
29 People working together
30 Suggestions from others
31 Numerical summary or average
32 An "equal" to you at work
35 To carefully hear what others say
37 To give council and suggestions
38 Scores needing improvement

Assessment

MULTIPOINT FEEDBACK

MULTIPOINT FEEDBACK
A 360° CATALYST FOR CHANGE

A FIFTY-MINUTE™ BOOK

The objectives of this book are:

1. to explain multipoint feedback and its usefulness.

2. to show how to administer multi-point feedback.

3. to explain the mechanics of a r multipoint feedback survey.

4. to discuss evaluation and implementation of a multipoint feedback survey.

Disclaimer:
These assessments were written to test the reader on the content of the book. They were not developed by a professional test writer. The publisher and author shall have neither liability nor responsibility to any person with respect to any loss or damage caused or alleged to be caused directly or indirectly by the assessment contained herein.

ASSESSMENT OBJECTIVE FOR MULTIPOINT FEEDBACK

Select the best response.

1. Multipoint feedback is a way to gain insight about your performance from
   A. your peers and customers.
   B. those you report to.
   C. yourself.
   D. all of the above.
   E. A and B.

2. Multipoint feedback is
   A. systematic, targeted and specific.
   B. casual, individualistic, and varied.

3. Change happens as a result of
   A. pain, inertia, thinking, planning.
   B. pain, seeing an ideal, taking steps.
   C. believing in older ways.

4. Identifying specific behavior changes that are needed is the first objective of the multipoint feedback process.
   A. True
   B. False

5. The multipoint feedback process must
   A. include written rather than mathematical feedback.
   B. solicit feedback from new employees.
   C. be used only for evaluation.
   D. all of the above.
   E. none of the above.

6. A multipoint survey should occur
   A. only once.
   B. three months after the first time.
   C. eighteen months after the first time.
   D. at intervals of at least six months.

7. Multipoint feedback should become a voice on the performance appraisal only after it is first used developmentally.
   A. True
   B. False

OBJECTIVE ASSESSMENT (continued)

8. The best facilitator of a multipoint feedback session should be
   A. a neutral outsider.
   B. a skilled manager.
   C. someone from another department.
   D. any interested person.

9. Data from a multipoint feedback instrument should be
   A. represented as average scores or ranges.
   B. anonymous.
   C. include specific names and departments.
   D. A and B.
   E. B and C.

10. A leadership model must be originated
    A. before the multipoint feedback survey is developed.
    B. based on the multipoint feedback results.

11. Desired behaviors should
    A. begin with a verb such as *provides*.
    B. include compound questions.
    C. be stated in at least 40 questions.
    D. all of the above.

12. An *off-the-shelf* multipoint feedback survey is best because
    A. it guarantees anonymity.
    B. relates exactly to your organization.
    C. it avoids favoring management.
    D. all of the above.
    E. none of the above.

13. An ideal range for a rating scale is
    A. 1–12.
    B. 1–5.
    C. 1–3.
    D. 1–10.

14. Participation in multipoint feedback should be
    A. optional for all employees.
    B. required of at least a few employees.
    C. required of all employees.
    D. required of new employees only.

15. Respondents tend to be more honest if written comments are
    A. not used.
    B. anonymous.
    C. stated in the respondent's exact words.
    D. A and B.
    E. B and C.

16. It is important to describe the purpose and uses of the multipoint feedback survey before it is taken.
    A. True
    B. False

17. The best return rate can be expected if respondents are asked to return their form in
    A. one week.
    B. two weeks.
    C. one day.
    D. any deadline.

18. Averaging scores is
    A. the best summary method.
    B. best if combined with distribution of scores.
    C. is inferior to distribution of scores.
    D. is seldom recommended.

19. Multipoint feedback reports
    A. may not be true.
    B. may be contradictory.
    C. are perceptions.
    D. should not be complex.
    E. all of the above.

20. When comparing your self-evaluation with others' evaluation of you, you should
    A. discount others' ideas that you believe are faulty.
    B. pay attention to gaps of one point or greater.
    C. consider averages rather than distributions.
    D. be sure all people asked to report have done so.
    E. all of the above.

OBJECTIVE ASSESSMENT (continued)

21. If you are surprised by some items in your feedback, you should
    A. try to understand why people might feel the way they do.
    B. brainstorm options for behavior change.
    C. imagine how to take advantage of your strengths.
    D. all of the above.
    E. none of the above.

22. A feedback meeting with your direct reports should
    A. involve only you and your direct reports.
    B. include a facilitator if your team has major complaints.
    C. concentrate only on strengths.
    D. concentrate only on opportunities for change.
    E. B and C.

23. The time allowed for a feedback meeting with your direct reports should be
    A. at least an hour.
    B. at least two hours.
    C. any length that is necessary.
    D. short and to the point.

24. When faced with areas needed for your improvement, you should
    A. explain why you have acted as you have.
    B. listen to the ideas of your direct reports without giving your own ideas.
    C. jointly negotiate a path forward.
    D. simply explain how you will change your behavior.

25. Once it is understood how your behavior should change in some areas, you should.
    A. try your best to change without talking about it.
    B. try sending out check-in cards in 4–6 months.
    C. regularly ask your direct reports how you are doing.
    D. try to avoid areas where you have been weak.

Qualitative Objectives for *Multipoint Feedback*

To explain multipoint feedback and its usefulness

Questions 1, 2, 3, 4, 5

To show how to administer multi-point feedback

Questions 6, 8, 12, 22

To explain the mechanics of a multipoint feedback survey

Questions 5, 9, 11, 13, 15, 17, 18

To discuss evaluation and implementation of a multipoint feedback survey

Questions 7, 10, 14, 16, 19, 20, 21, 23, 24, 25

Answer Key

1. D	**10.** A	**18.** B
2. A	**11.** A	**19.** E
3. B	**12.** E	**20.** B
4. A	**13.** B	**21.** D
5. E	**14.** A	**22.** B
6. D	**15.** B	**23.** B
7. A	**16.** A	**24.** C
8. A	**17.** B	**25.** B
9. D		

Copyright © 1997, Crisp Publications, Inc.
1200 Hamilton Court
Menlo Park, California 94025

NOTES

NOTES

NOTES

NOTES

NOTES

NOTES

NOTES